CHARLOTTE'S WEB AND THE GOSPEL

Leon Collier

Copyright © 2016

Published in the United States of America

COPYRIGHT DISCLAIMER

All Rights Reserved. Reproduction or transmission in any form of any part of this document, mechanical or electronically, including photocopying, recording or by any information storage and retrieval system beyond that permitted in Section 107 or 108 of the 1976 United States Copyright Act is unlawful without the expressed written permission of the copyright author and publisher. International copyright laws also apply.

Charlotte's Web and The Gospel
First Edition, Paperback
Published Date: December 2019
Alpha Academic Press
ISBN: 978-1-948210-10-2

Table of Contents

Introduction 7
Chapter 1
  A Pig's Salvation 9
Chapter 2
  Identity Metamorphosis 13
Chapter 3
  Divine Vocation 19
Chapter 4
  Success against All Odds 25
Bibliography 29

Introduction

In the early years of my life, I recall watching *Charlotte's Web* on television and fell in love with the story. In December 2006, *Charlotte's Web* hit the big screen for the first time since its inception. E.B. White's story inspired a new generation. The kids were out of school for the holidays, and my wife and I decided to take our three daughters, Noel, Leona and Leondria, to see *Charlotte's Web*. They were ecstatic about the movie, and my heart brimmed over with extraordinary bliss about spending time with my family. As I watched the movie with forty-four-year-old clergy eyes, my theological radar went off numerous times as I detected some life lessons taught by a little eight-year-old girl name Fern, a pig named Wilbur and a spider named Charlotte, along with a host of other farm animals.

I leaned over to Yolanda and said, "Hey, there are many lessons to be learned from this movie."

"Do you feel like God is speaking to you?" she asked.

"Yes," I replied. "What God wants me to say about this story will become clearer in time."

About a week later, I awoke around 5:30 A.M. and as I lay in bed thinking, I had what could be deemed an inspired moment. As I thought about the story, all of a sudden out of my inner well of insight, four words surfaced that summed up the story in its entirety. The words *salvation*, *identification*, *vocation* and *destination* came to mind. Immediately, I got up and wrote them down with all certainty that the sermon God had given me about this story would be centered on these four words.

I felt led to study the story more closely, so a few days later I went to Books-A-Million and purchased the book. My intentions were to read the story and find situations in the book that related to those four words, and the following information transpired as a result.

Chapter 1

A Pig's Salvation

I usually study and prepare for Sunday sermons on Thursday and Friday, and when the time came to craft my four themes into a book, my approach was simple: take each word and match it up with a biblical text to show how they relate. The first word I dealt with was *salvation*. This word was given first because the story begins with the salvation of a little runt pig named Wilbur. The first sentence in the book reads, "Where's Papa going with the ax?"[1]

Fern's father was on his way to the hog house with an ax to kill a runt pig that was considered to have little chance of surviving, but Fern was determined to save the runt pig. Fern's father, Mr. Arable, was equally tenacious about killing the pig, which resulted in a tense battle of words between the two. Fern was young, but as it turned out she was well-prepared for the task at hand. Her resolve and convincing argument garnered the mercy of her father, and the runt pig's life was spared for a season.

I grew up in a rural community in the late 1960s and early 70s, and I am well acquainted with pig pens and the stench that comes with them. The pig pen is symbolic of the world, considering its social ills and immorality, but God is gracious and full of mercy. However, he is also just and holy, and therefore, sin must be accounted for. Mr. Arable is a type of God who came to the hog house (sinful world) with an axe to get rid of weak, runty pigs (sinners). Fern cried that it was unjust to kill the pig just because it was a runt. It was not the pig's fault it was born that way. She even fiercely grabbed hold of the axe and would not let go, which is symbolic of Christ's passion and sacrifice for us.

Jesus stood in our defense on the cross because even though we were guilty of our personal sins, it was not our fault we have a sin nature passed on to us by Adam and Eve. For that reason, Jesus was willing to stand in the gap (hold on to the axe) and plead our case by His shed blood; and just as Mr. Arable listened to Fern, God listened to Jesus and gave us life rather than death. The Apostle Paul said, "But God commended his love toward us, in that, while we were yet sinners, Christ died for us" (Rom 5:8 KJV).

It amazes me how pessimistic people can be at times. Fern's mother, Mrs. Arable, agreed with Mr. Arable. "It's [pig] very small and weak and it will never amount to anything anyway."[2]

A familiar saying of our day is, "Don't let anybody tell you it can't be done." This saying was birthed out of the sea of negativism that exists in the world. In the movie "The Color Purple," Celli's treacherous and abusive husband criticized her when she made up her mind to leave. He implied that she would never make it because she was poor, black, a woman and ugly. Wilbur the pig came into the world under such deplorable pretext, but Fern came to his rescue. Similarly, we were without hope until God sent Jesus to the cross.

Of course, Fern is not the only character in the story who is a type of Christ. As Wilber grew, Charlotte the spider helped extend his life, also. However, once again Wilbur found himself amidst severe negativism. Two accounts of words of discouragement come to mind. One is when Templeton had made a night of indulging in the spoils of the fair. Charlotte criticized him for gorging himself and implied that it would serve him right if he got an acute case of indigestion. Templeton was not one to remain silent, especially under such scrutiny, and he sneeringly told Charlotte to not worry about his stomach. In other words, mind your own business. After setting Charlotte straight, he turned his attention to Wilbur and blasted him with some very bad news. He brought to his attention that the larger pig in the stall next door had a blue ribbon, which meant that Wilbur had lost the competition and that Mr. Zuckerman might change his mind about Wilbur, and when Zuckerman developed a craving for some crisp bacon, he would take the knife to Wilbur.

Earlier in the story, the goose told Wilbur that he did not envy him, because at the arrival of winter he (Wilbur) would be killed and turned into smoked ham. Obviously, this highly upset Wilbur, but Charlotte promised him that she would find a way to help him live. I find it interesting that Charlotte saved Wilbur by weaving words in her web. Charlotte wove words that drew attention to Wilbur and made him special in the eyes of humans in the same way God sent Jesus, who is the WORD (Jn 1:1, 14), into the world to save us. Words are powerful and can render life or death. King Solomon said, "Death and life are in the power of the tongue" (Prv 18:21a-RSV). He also said, "For they are life to him who finds them, and healing to all his flesh" (Prv 4:22 RSV).

Wilbur's life was secured by the words Charlotte wove in her web, and it is by the word of God (Jesus) that our souls are spared.

The pivotal point regarding the word *salvation* in this story is a conversation that took place between Charlotte and Wilbur. Charlotte's life as a spider was rapidly coming to a close, and Wilbur noticed that she was a bit sluggish and asked her if she was alright. Charlotte rendered a tremendous discourse of victory concerning the future of Wilbur's life. Afterwards, Wilbur asked Charlotte why she made all the sacrifices for him, because he didn't feel worthy. I find Charlotte's response most interesting: "I wove my webs for you because I liked you."[3]

Likewise, we could ask the same question of Jesus Christ. We know we are not worthy. Why did you make all the sacrifices for us? With all certainty, Jesus' reply is, "I went to the cross for you because I love you." Although we were in a hog house (sin) and on our way to the smoke house (hell) and well deserved it, Jesus stepped in and paid the price for our sins. Why did He do it? *I wove my webs for you because I love you.*

Chapter 2

Identity Metamorphosis

In the fourth sentence of the first chapter of *Charlotte's Web*, Wilbur is identified. "Well," said her mother, "one of the pigs is **a runt**. It's very small and weak, and it will never amount to anything."4

Mr. Arable was about to put the ax to Wilbur, but Fern stood in its defense. Fern's father had a negative view of Wilbur at the time. In fact, he said that a weakling makes trouble, and he went on to say that a little girl is one thing, but a little runty pig is another. By grace Wilbur escaped the destruction of the ax, but as life would have it, his endeavor to live proved to be an uphill battle. One day, the old sheep walked into the barn yard to pay Wilbur a visit. He alluded to Wilbur's weight gain, which Wilbur implied was a good thing for a pig. However, the old sheep made it crystal clear that he did not envy him, because for a pig to gain weight meant that by winter the farmers would kill him and turn him into crisp bacon and ham. Therefore, Wilbur was identified as a spring pig, which meant he would be winter bacon. Of course, the other characters were identified in certain ways in the beginning of the story, also.

In the motion picture about *Charlotte's Web*, the horse was dreadfully afraid of the spider and could not stand to be in its presence nor even look at it. The geese, the lambs and the cows were very opinionated and often negative. The most detestable characters were the flies. No one had anything good to say about them because they spent the majority of their time being a nuisance to the cows, sheep and horses, and the farmers often complained about them. If this was not bad enough, the spider trapped them in her web and ate them. No matter how much the flies were hated, they yet served a purpose. The flies made it possible for all of the characters to agree on something. They all loathed the flies. Perhaps this is why God allows flies (problems) in our lives at times. He knows that flies create an atmosphere to enhance patience and a resilient prayer life.

Wilbur admitted that his first impression of Charlotte was that she was cruel and bloodthirsty. True to form, Templeton the rat identified himself. At one point in time, Wilbur was bored and wanted someone to play with, and the following response identifies Templeton perfectly. "I never do those things if I can avoid them," replied the rat, sourly. "I prefer to spend my time eating, gnawing, spying, and hiding. I am a glutton but not a merrymaker. Right now I am on my way to your trough to eat your breakfast, since you haven't got sense enough to eat it yourself."[5]

Obviously, the identification of these characters is negative at the beginning of the story. This reminds me of a biblical character named Gideon who had a negative view of himself. He saw himself as God-forsaken (Jgs 6:13), he saw his family as the poorest in his tribe and he thought of himself as the least in his family (Jgs 6:15). Many people fail to reach their maximum potential because they have a poor self-image and are in need of a major identity metamorphosis. They have hidden talents that have not been tapped into, which leads to great success once discovered and utilized. God will send people into our path to help us discover those talents, and thereby reach our full potential.

The angel showed up in Gideon's situation and pronounced his ultimate identity (Jgs 6:12, 14). Notice the angel called him brave and a savior for his people. Gideon saw himself as a farmer, but God created him to be a brave worrier who had the potential to deliver his people from the fear and bondage of their enemies (Midianites). Your identity was given to you before you were born, and with God's help you can discover your identity and purpose.

In the story of *Charlotte's Web*, Wilbur was graciously assisted by Charlotte in discovering who he really was as opposed to who he thought he was at the beginning of the story. Having been made aware of his coming doom, Wilbur felt terribly lonely and sobbed bitterly. When darkness covered the barn yard and the sounds of the night permeated the surroundings, a life-changing moment took place for Wilbur. Amidst the loneliness and darkness chimed a beautiful, emaciated voice that asked Wilbur if he wanted a friend. Charlotte volunteered her friendship at a time when Wilbur needed it the most. She had been watching him for a while and decided that this was the perfect time to approach him.

Likewise, God is watching over us, and when things get really bad, he sends people into our lives when we need them most. The angel's timing was perfect in Gideon's case because his people had been terrorized by the Midianites for some time, and perhaps he had all he could take. The angel redefined Gideon's life as Charlotte redefined Wilbur's life. Who you are today will not be who you are going to be in the future if you accept God's offer of friendship.

One day when Wilbur was lamenting over his future destruction, screaming he did not want to die, Charlotte comforted him by promising him he would not depart this life, because she would find a way to save him. Sure enough, she used her web to help spare Wilbur's life. She wove words that drew attention to him in a positive way. The first words she wove were "Some Pig." This implied that Wilbur was special. In what way was he special (some pig)? After all, he was born an insignificant runt; therefore, his being special had very little to do with him. What made him special is when Fern stood up for him, thereby saving his life. He could have been killed at birth, but grace kept him alive; this alone is what made him "Some Pig." We are special because of what God has done for us, and it has nothing to do with us (Eph 2:8, 9).

The next word Charlotte wove to identify Wilbur was "Terrific." However, Wilbur did not think he was terrific. Sometimes it is hard for us to see what others see in us. Indeed, Wilbur was terrific because he inspired the other farm animals to love others unlike themselves, and he was the reason they united for a worthwhile cause.

As the story progressed, some of the characters experienced an identity metamorphosis. Rather than spewing ever-flowing words of Wilbur's doom, the farm animals rallied together to find a way to save Wilbur's life. Of course, Templeton the rat implied that he could care less, until he was reminded that his survival depended upon Wilbur's survival since he ate from Wilbur's trough every day. No matter how blessed we are, we must depend on others because our survival depends on the survival of others. Therefore, extreme independence is detrimental and can leave us alienated from people and God, all of whom we need to survive.

Be that as it may, Templeton was convinced that he needed to look for a magazine clipping during his next trip to the dump. Later, when the rat returned from the dump, the word he gave Charlotte was unacceptable, and she said they must use a word that advertises

Wilbur's noble qualities. So Templeton returned to the dump once again, but the word he chose was rejected by Charlotte again. At this point, the rat was frustrated and implied that Charlotte had defined him as a messenger boy. This was exactly the case. The rat was not just a selfish farmyard parasite but now played a very important role as a messenger boy to help save the pig. This was certainly an identity metamorphosis for Templeton although he detested it.

Mr. Zuckerman decided to take Wilbur to the fair and enter him in a contest. He had Lurvy clean up a crate and write in big green letters, "Zuckerman's Famous Pig." Wilbur had experienced an identity metamorphosis, also. In fact, Wilbur's identity metamorphosis is most significant of all the farm animals because he started out a runty pig about to be axed, a runty pig sold for a measly six dollars, and became a spring pig destined for the smoke house (bacon); but later he was named "Some Pig," "Terrific," "Zuckerman's Famous Pig" and "Humble," and was finally a prize-winning pig.

I fancy the way E.B. White identified Wilbur in the end as humble. Wilbur had gone through a lot during his lifetime, but in the end, grace placed him in a most favorable position. It was at this point that humility was the final word to describe Wilbur. What a tremendous lesson for us all: No matter how much success we achieve, humility is always appropriate.

Identity metamorphosis can bring about freedom. I recall the goose who talked Wilbur into bursting out of the barnyard, and when Wilbur did so, the goose asked what it felt like to be free. Then he told Wilbur all the wonderful things he could do and finally said, "The world is a wonderful place when you are young." Replace the word *young* with the word *free. The world is a wonderful place when you are free.* The world is a wonderful place when you know who you are, because it gives you a sense of freedom. Mother Teresa was surrounded by extreme poverty in Calcutta, India, but she was free because she knew who she was and what role she was chosen to play.

Charlotte also experienced identity metamorphosis. Wilbur's first impression of Charlotte was that she was cruel and bloodthirsty, but in the end he discovered that she was very giving, supportive and willing to make great sacrifices for those she loved. Of course, Charlotte alluded to her own identity. "After all, what's life, anyway? We're born, we live a little while, we die. A spider's life can't help being something of a mess, with all this trapping and eating flies. By helping you (Wilbur), perhaps I was trying to lift up my life a trifle."[6]

She saw herself differently because she had a highly esteemed purpose when Wilbur came along. Helping Wilbur gave her a sense of dignity and duty. Perhaps this is something for the human race to consider, that life is not worth living unless you help others.

As I bring the matter of identity metamorphosis to a close, we now return to the beginning of the story where Fern is holding the axe of her father, Mr. Arable, to keep him from killing Wilbur. Fern said, "If I had been born very small at birth, would you have killed me?" "Certainly not," he said…"But this is different. A little girl is one thing; a little runty pig is another." "I see no difference," replied Fern, still hanging on to the ax.[7]

The words *I see no difference* stand out in my mind because this reminds me of those who are Christians. Fern is a type of Christ, who held back the ax in our defense, and when He died on the cross, His shed blood covered our sins. Jesus now stands beside us, and when God looks at us and Jesus, He says, "I see no difference" (Col 1:22; 2 Cor 5:21). This is our new identity.

Chapter 3

Divine Vocation

When Wilbur received the bad news about his upcoming slaughter, he wept bitterly, but Charlotte assured him that she would help him, and her endeavor to save Wilbur proved to be a worthwhile and divine vocation.

One's natural ability is a part of one's divine vocation; therefore, one is required to exercise it when needed. In *Charlotte's Web*, all of the characters had certain vocations. Mr. Arable, Mrs. Arable, Mr. Zuckerman and Mrs. Zuckerman were farmers. Lurvey was a hired hand for the Zuckermans. Fern Arable's vocation was to take care of the runty pig (Wilbur). My impression of Fern's brother is that most of the time he goofed around and always wanted what Fern had. A perfect example is when Fern was given a pig—he wanted one, also. This is the sad reality of some people. They don't want to commit to something and stick with it; however, they want what others have.

The flies' vocation was simply to pester everyone. The larger purpose of their vocation was to make people stronger and help them stay focused amidst distractions.

Templeton's vocation was not simply to rummage through trash and pack stuff in his rat hole, but the larger purpose of his vocation was to grope through debris to find words that would help save Wilbur the pig. Perhaps all vocations should be viewed as a means to enhance the lives of others. Charlotte the spider wove webs, but she did not weave webs just to catch flies. The larger purpose for her weaving webs was to save a life. Likewise, the larger purpose of our vocations is to improve the quality of life of others. Finally, Wilbur's vocation was to eat slop, gain weight, root up dirt and roll around in mud all day. Humorously speaking, a pig's life appears to be one big vacation (vocation). However, the larger purpose of Wilbur's vocation shows that a runt pig that had a close brush with death became a prize-winning pig and outlived all of his siblings. All the farm animals were given a single vocation, which was to help save Wilbur. Therefore, Wilbur's vocation also included existing as a pig threatened by potential death, thus giving the other farm animals the single purpose of saving a friend (Wilbur).

As I reflected upon the vocation of the characters three things came to mind: **Attitude in vocation, vocational confusion** and the **necessity of vocation**. What should our attitudes be when it comes to vocation? Obviously, there is a **wrong and a right attitude** regarding this matter. Templeton is the best example of the wrong attitude when it comes to vocation. He was always negative and often complained about having to search for words, implying that he was not a messenger boy. One instance was when Templeton made a night of plundering the spoils of the fair and stuffed himself shamelessly. Charlotte callously criticized him, and his response was negative as usual.

"Don't worry about my stomach," snarled Templeton. "It can handle anything. And by the way, I've got some bad news. As I came past that pig next door—the one that calls himself Uncle—I noticed a blue tag on the front of his pen. That means he has won first prize. I guess you are licked, Wilbur. You might as well relax—nobody is going to hang a medal on you. Furthermore, I wouldn't be surprised if Zuckerman changes his mind about you. Wait till he gets hankering for some fresh pork and smoked ham and crisp bacon! He'll take the knife to you, my boy."[8]

I admit that Templeton's words are somewhat hilarious. Obviously, going to the fair to help Wilbur was not Templeton's main motivation. His sole purpose for tagging along with Wilbur and Charlotte to the fair was so he could have his way with the spoils, and after gorging himself all night long, his morning greeting consisted of pessimistic news. Templeton serves as a picture-perfect example of some people who have the wrong attitude when it comes to their vocation. They are not interested in helping people, but they are more interested in serving self and will not serve others unless there is something in it for them.

Charlotte the spider best reflects the right attitude when it comes to vocation. She actually liked Wilbur, which is why she wanted to help him. The Apostle Paul reminded the Christian community what kind of attitude they should have when giving: "Let each man give according as he has determined in his heart; not grudgingly, or under compulsion; for God loves a cheerful giver." (2 Cor 9:7 WEB) This proves that having the right attitude when serving ranks high with God. The wrong attitude disqualifies the work, as well as the worker, in God's eyes. Cain's offering was rejected because he had the wrong attitude (no faith) (Heb 11:4).

Charlotte liked Wilbur, and it was reflected in her work. She did an excellent job of weaving words on his behalf. Sometimes, the depth of our love for God is reflected in the quality of service we render to Him.

One final point regarding having the right attitude in vocation is being able to stay focused on the task at hand amidst disruptions. When Charlotte's life as a spider was coming to a close, she told Wilbur her life was languishing, and Wilbur asked her what that meant. She responded, "It means I'm slowing up, feeling my age. I'm not young anymore, Wilbur. But I don't want you to worry about me. This is your big day today. Look at my web—doesn't it show up well with the dew on it?"[9]

Charlotte stayed focused on the big picture. She did not allow her personal situation to sway from and belittle the main issue. She made her vocation the chief focus. What a tremendous lesson taught by this spider! Similarly, Jesus did not make His intense suffering the main issue on the cross. He made people the issue when He said, "Father, forgive them; for they know not what they do" (Lk 23:34 ASV). Even when attacked unfairly by one of the thieves who was crucified beside Him, He yet remained focused on His vocation.

The soldiers mocked Him: "And the soldiers also mocked him, coming to him, offering him vinegar, and saying, If thou art the King of the Jews, save thyself" (Lk 23:36, 37 ASV). One of the thieves mocked Him: "And one of the malefactors that were hanged railed on him, saying, Art not thou the Christ? Save thyself and us" (Lk 23:39 ASV). Notwithstanding the ridicule, the Lord ignored the unfair treatment and rather chose to give attention to the vocation at hand:

But the other answered, and rebuking him said, Dost thou not even fear God, seeing thou art in the same condemnation? And we indeed justly; for we receive the due reward of our deeds: but this man hath done nothing amiss. And he said, Jesus, remember me when thou comest in thy kingdom. And he said unto him, Verily I say unto thee, To-day shalt thou be with me in Paradise.

—Luke 23:40-43 ASV

Jesus realized the greater purpose at hand; therefore, having been mistreated took less precedence than His vocation. Jesus placed helping those who wanted help above the personal injustices He encountered. He faced both unfairness and vocation simultaneously, and He chose vocation. Perhaps we all could do a better job if we maintained such an attitude.

The second concern I have apropos occupation is **vocational confusion**. They took Wilbur to the fair in a crate, and once they removed him, Fern's brother, Avery, jumped inside on all fours and emulated a pig. Without a doubt, Avery looked pretty stupid. Whenever people try to do what God did not call them to do nor gifted them to do, they look foolish. There is a saying that goes, "You can do anything you want to do if you put your mind to it." This couldn't be further from the truth. God gave you certain abilities, but there are some things you will never be able to do because God did not give you the capability to do them. I am reminded of a funny scene in a comedy TV show. One man said he always remembered that saying, "If at first you do not succeed, try and try again." The other man responded, "Don't believe that. People say that so losers won't kill themselves." You must admit this is funny.

The truth is we can save ourselves from much heartache if we do what God has called and gifted us to do. Wilbur foolishly boasted to Charlotte that he could spin a web if she showed him how to do it. Wilbur had Templeton attach a string to his tail and he climbed on top of a dung hill and leaped into the air and landed in the pile of manure. When people try to do what God did not call nor gifted them to do, sooner or later they find themselves in a pile of droppings. Wilbur wasted his time trying to do what Charlotte was created to do. Finally, Charlotte told Wilbur that he didn't have to spin webs to catch his food, because his food was brought to him everyday. Trying to do what you are not gifted to do sends the wrong message. It says you don't appreciate the gifts/talents God has given you. Don't try to be like someone else; be who God created you to be and do what God created you to do. Focus on what you can do and try to be the best at it.

My final crucial point on the subject of vocation is **the necessity of it**. Near the end of the story, Wilbur asked Charlotte why she did all this for him, and she responded, "After all, what's a life, anyway? We're born, we live a little, we die. A spider's life can't help being something of a mess, with all this trapping and eating flies. By helping you, perhaps I was trying to lift up my life a trifle. Heaven knows anyone's life can stand a little of that."[10]

Charlotte's life and work was given worth because she helped Wilbur. If all you do is serve yourself, your life and work is reduced to trapping flies and living a life of trifle. In God's eyes, it's not what you do for self that matters; it's what you do for others that counts the most. One of Jesus' famous quotes says, "For the Son of Man also came not to be served, but to serve, and to give his life as a ransom for many" (Mk 10:45 WEB). However, there are blessings that automatically come when we unselfishly serve others. The sheep convinced Templeton to go to the fair with Charlotte and Wilbur. The rat adamantly refused at first, until the sheep told him about all the goodies he could encounter. Templeton went to the fair and found the final word Charlotte needed to seal the deal for Wilbur's fate. As it turned out, Templeton discovered that the sheep was right about all the spoils at the fair. He said, "The old sheep was right—this fair is a rat's paradise. What eating! And what drinking! And everywhere good hiding and good hunting. Bye, bye, my humble Wilbur! Fare thee well, Charlotte, you old schemer! This will be a night to remember in a rat's life."[11]

Templeton grudgingly went to the fair, but he went anyway and did his part and was blessed as a result. John Wesley said, "Do all the good you can by all the means you can, in all the ways you can, in all the places you can, to all the people you can, as long as ever you can."

I would like to end the subject of vocation with Charlotte's words to Wilbur about her work of completing the egg sack. "It's my egg sack, my magnum opus." "What's that?" asked Wilbur. "The word is Latin and it means *great work*. The egg sack is my great work—the finest thing I have ever made."[12]

I am reminded of what Jesus said about the two servants who worked hard at investing the talents their master gave them. When their work was evaluated the master said: "... Well done, good and faithful servant" (Mt 25:21 ASV).

We should give our very best in whatever we do so that when our work is appraised we will hear with joy the words "Magnum Opus."

Chapter 4

Success against All Odds

Now we come to the final stage of Wilbur's destiny in life, and what a joy it has been to watch him go through various phases of life, many of which were intensely difficult. However, by divine grace and undying love and support of genuine friends, Wilbur succeeded against all odds. The threat of death at birth, the loneliness in the dark and the frightening words of bloody slaughter only served as stepping stones to becoming a celebrated, prize-winning pig. I am reminded of a scene in the Bible where certain people suffered and were killed during turbulent times. However, in the end they were celebrated for their sacrifice and faith (Rev 7:9, 13-17).

After these things I looked, and behold, a great multitude which no one could number, of all nations, tribes, peoples, and tongues, standing before the throne and before the Lamb, clothed with white robes, with palm branches in their hands, and crying out with a loud voice, saying, "Salvation belongs to our God who sits on the throne, and to the Lamb!"

—Revelation 7:9, 10 NKJV

The Greek word for *cried* in this verse is *krazo,* which means "to scream." They shouted because they were in the presence of Jesus and because of all the trials they had endured. It was a time of celebration. Likewise, Wilbur fainted in the presence of the crowd, overwhelmed by sheer excitement and the prize he was about to receive. Perhaps flashes of the past dashing through his mind only made him more excited, having reminisced that his chances of ever becoming a prize-winning pig was indeed non-existent in the beginning. Wilbur's life started out with death threats that forecasted his demise, but in the final analysis, by grace longevity proved otherwise.

Christians can relate to this in that we were once threatened with eternal damnation, but through Christ we have eternal life. There are numerous biblical narratives that reflect this idea. Moses was born in a dark social environment that landed him in a basket floating on the Nile River. By the way, the word *Nile* means "dark, and it is also referred to in the Old Testament as Sihor, which means "the black stream." That is how Moses' life started, but the latter part of his life brought him face to face with water once again. He led the children of Israel to the Red Sea.

Some Bible scholars think the Greeks called the sea Red because the zoophytes that floated on the water were reddish. Obviously, red is a bright color. Notice the sea he floated on in a basket when he was a child means dark (Nile), but the river he passed through to freedom means red (bright). God has a bright future for all people, and if we are willing to labor and trust him, dark days will one day transform into bright successes. Like Wilbur, we, too, will discover that all the suffering, hard work and patience are worthwhile.

The subjects in Revelation chapter seven mirrors this perfectly:

They shall neither hunger anymore nor thirst anymore; the sun shall not strike them, nor any heat; for the Lamb who is in the midst of the throne will shepherd them and lead them to living fountains of waters. And God will wipe away every tear from their eyes. (NKJV)

This reminds me of Charlotte's words to Wilbur. "Your future is assured. You will live, secure and safe, Wilbur. Nothing can harm you now...Christmas will come, then the snows of winter...Winter will pass, the days will lengthen, the ice will melt in the pasture pond. The song sparrow will return and sing, the frogs will awake, the warm wind will blow again. All these sights and sounds and smells will be yours to enjoy."[13]

Though the people in the Book of Revelation chapter seven suffered dearly, the prize was worth every ounce of anguish they endured. The Apostle Paul said it best: "For I consider that the sufferings of this present time are not worthy to be compared with the glory which shall be revealed in us" (Rom 8:18 NKJV).

The people in Revelation 7:9 were given white robes and palm branches. The white robes represent purity, and the palm branches symbolize victory. They had finally reached their glorious destination. Likewise, Wilbur was given a prize. One of the judges tied a medal around his neck. This was more than just a celebration of some magnificent, humble pig. The prize symbolized victory over death at birth, as well as victory over death as a spring pig. Mr. Arable intended one thing, but the grace of God intended another. The love of God is reflected throughout the story of *Charlotte's Web*, and we can draw from its well of grace and find abundant encouragement to keep on going no matter what the odds may be, because in the end, by God's amazing grace we will reach our destination.

I recall my high school years, much of which was spent in the shadow of my popular, older siblings. My brother Sammie was extremely good in football and became well known for his athletic prowess. Likewise, my sister Barbra was an outstanding, record-setting track star, a high-scoring basketball player and a dominant force on her debate team. By the time I made it to high school, I found myself engulfed in their shadows. In the tenth grade, I decided to try my hand at track and field; however, I had one weakness. I was not small enough to be a legitimate miler and not quite fast enough to be an exceptional sprinter. I was caught in between, just as I was sandwiched by my popular siblings.

Deep within the recesses of my mind, from time to time, I got upset for being known as Sammie and Barbra Collier's little brother, but there was nothing I could do about it. I could only wish things were different. When I entered eleventh grade, I rededicated my life to Christ and by God's amazing grace, a year later my fate changed. One unforgettable morning in my first period class, one of my classmates told me I was nominated to be on the Who's Who ballet for "Most Likely to Succeed." My initial reaction was one of disbelief; however, when it became clear to me that it was really true, my soul was sated with jubilation. I could not wait to tell my mother and siblings the good news and when I shared the news with them they were very excited about the possibility. My time had finally arrived, I thought, and if I ended up being selected as "Most Likely to Succeed" for the Class of 1980 of Starkville High School, this would propel me from underneath the shadows of my siblings.

While waiting for that great day I was inspired, because during that time I felt in my heart that God would allow me to be selected so my life could be a reflection of his glory. I told my sister, Barbra, that I had an inspired feeling that I would be crowned with the honor, without a shadow of a doubt. While I firmly held this belief as the day of Who's

Who drew near, I must admit butterflies saturated my stomach. My fear apexed on that great day when I sat beside Tony Alexander in the gym, awaiting the announcement of who won the "Most Likely to Succeed" title. Tony was arguably one of the smartest students at Starkville High School and was nominated for the same honor. I recall him smiling as I glanced at him nervously smiling back. Somehow, I sensed he really meant me well, effortlessly giving an air of tremendous security, having fared well in academics.

Finally, there was total silence as the nominees for "Most Likely to Succeed" were read. "And the winner for Most likely to Succeed for the Class of 1980 is…LEON COLLIER," said the announcer. I was so excited I felt like running and jumping, but I tried to look cool. So I got up calmly and went to center court, bowed my head to receive the medal and took my place among the elite of Starkville High School for the first time. I slowly looked around in total elation with a deep sense of accomplishment. I officially had my own identification and had graduated from the shadows of my siblings. In fact, I felt my honor superseded all of their honors, because my classmates believed I was going to succeed in the future. Thus, my honor went beyond the present, unlike other honors, which is why I believed it was more significant than many of the honors of my siblings. Like Wilbur, I was assured that it does not matter how you start, but what really counts is how you finish.

A mother lost her teenage son of great promise and potential to an act of robbery and murder, and when she gave her remarks at his funeral her words were so profound they were carved into my memory. "It does not matter how long you live, but what matters is how well you live," she said. It does not matter where you have been but rather where you are headed that carries more weight.

In closing, I thank E.B. White for creating *Charlotte's Web* because it inspired me to write this little book, and I hope it motivates all who read it and leads them to reread *Charlotte's Web* and see it in a completely different light.

Bibliography

1. Charlotte's Web, E.B. White 1952, p. 1
2. Ibid p. 1
3. Ibid p. 164
4. Ibid p. 1
5. Ibid pp. 29, 30
6. Ibid p. 164
7. Ibid p. 3
8. Ibid p. 148
9. Ibid p. 146
10. Ibid p. 164
11. Ibid p. 140
12. Ibid pp. 144, 145
13. Ibid pp. 1163, 164